HOW THE
HUMAN
BODY WORKS

The Muscular System

By Simon Rose

MEDIA ENHANCED BOOKS
AV²
BY WEIGL™
ADDED VALUE · AUDIO VISUAL

www.av2books.com

AV² provides enriched content that supplements and complements this book. Weigl's AV² books strive to create inspired learning and engage young minds in a total learning experience.

Your AV² Media Enhanced books come alive with...

Audio
Listen to sections of the book read aloud.

Key Words
Study vocabulary, and complete a matching word activity.

Video
Watch informative video clips.

Quizzes
Test your knowledge.

Go to www.av2books.com, and enter this book's unique code.

BOOK CODE

P479920

Embedded Weblinks
Gain additional information for research.

Slide Show
View images and captions, and prepare a presentation.

AV² by Weigl brings you media enhanced books that support active learning.

Try This!
Complete activities and hands-on experiments.

... and much, much more!

Published by AV² by Weigl
350 5th Avenue, 59th Floor
New York, NY 10118
Websites: www.av2books.com   www.weigl.com

Library of Congress Cataloging in Publication Data Available on Request

ISBN 978-1-4896-1170-3 (hardcover)
ISBN 978-1-4896-1171-0 (softcover)
ISBN 978-1-4896-1172-7 (single-user eBook)
ISBN 978-1-4896-1173-4 (multi-user eBook)

Printed in the United States of America in North Mankato, Minnesota
1 2 3 4 5 6 7 8 9 0   18 17 16 15 14

062014
WEP090514

Project Coordinator Aaron Carr
Art Director Terry Paulhus

Contents

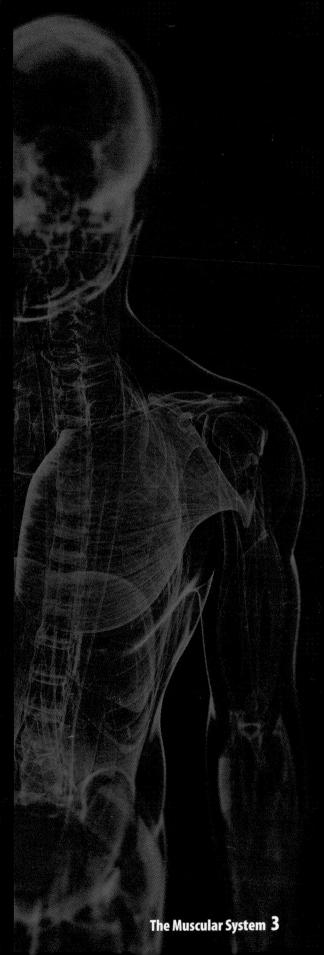

Human Body Systems

The human body is made up of complex systems. Each one plays an important role in how the body works. The systems are also interconnected. This means they work together.

For the body to stay healthy, its systems need to work together properly. Weakness or disease in a system can cause problems in one or more of the others. Often, more severe conditions in one system affect a greater number of other systems.

MUSCULAR SYSTEM

Supports and protects the skeletal system

Works closely with the nervous system to control how the body moves

Helps circulate blood and oxygen to keep the body alive

Is active in many **organs** and determines how they function

Gives the body strength and motion

6 MAJOR BODY SYSTEMS

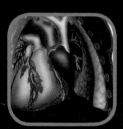

CARDIOVASCULAR SYSTEM

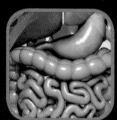

DIGESTIVE SYSTEM

MUSCULAR SYSTEM

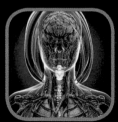

NERVOUS SYSTEM

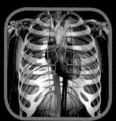

RESPIRATORY SYSTEM

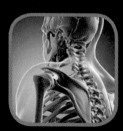

SKELETAL SYSTEM

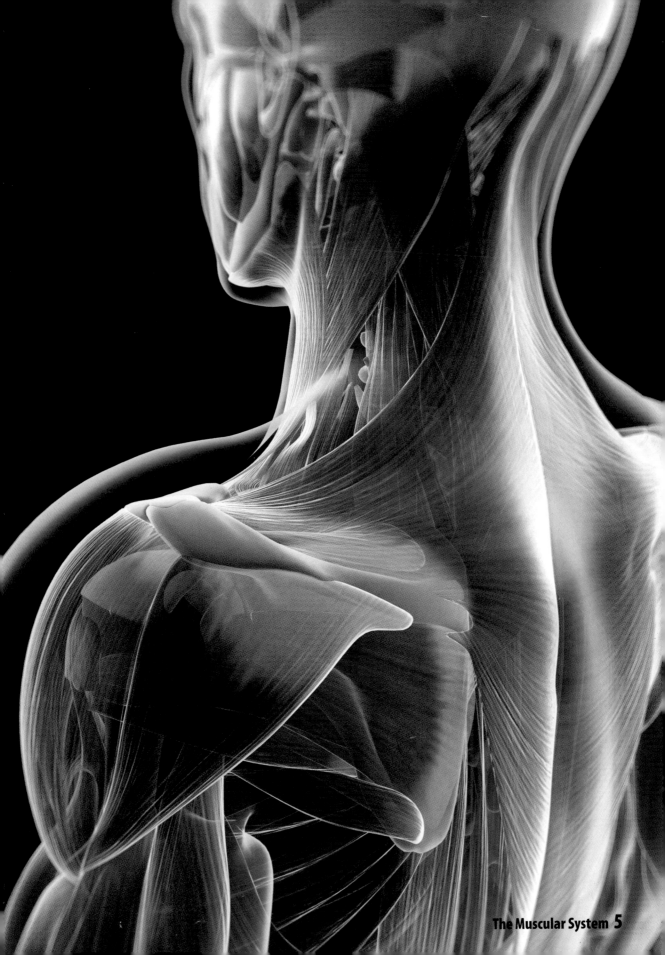

The Muscular System **5**

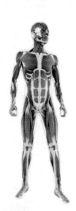

What Is the Muscular System?

The muscular system is made up of hundreds of muscles. They are bands or bundles of **fibers**. Muscles are elastic. They stretch and **contract** like rubber bands. The main function of muscles is movement. Some move body parts. Without these muscles, the body could not bend, stretch, twist, or turn. Also, a person without muscles could not stand, sit upright, or hold any part of the body in a certain position. Other muscles move substances such as blood and food throughout the body and help the body get rid of waste. Some muscles hold body parts in place. The body's nervous system controls the actions of muscles.

About half of a person's body weight is muscle. It is approximately three times as dense as fat, so a pound of muscle is only one-third the size of a pound of fat. People who train, or exercise, with heavy weights are able to increase their body weight because they are decreasing body fat and increasing muscle.

A person uses muscles in every part of the body even just to stand still.

There are between
600 and **700**
muscles in the body.

At **ONLY** 0.05 inches
(1.27 millimeters) long, the
stapedius muscle in the ear is the
SMALLEST
muscle in the human body.

The eye muscles make
10,000
movements in an
hour of reading.

A person uses about
17
muscles to
SMILE

The heart muscle contracts,
or beats, an average of
70
times per minute.

The heart muscle pumps
5 quarts
(4.7 liters) of blood
every minute.

The length of the body's
LONGEST
muscle, the sartorius, is
23.6 inches (600 mm).

Muscular System Features

The human body has three different types of muscles. Skeletal muscles are attached to bones and help them move. Smooth muscles are found in organs, such as the **esophagus**, intestines, and lungs. They are not attached to bones. Cardiac muscle is found only in the heart.

FRONTALIS Covers the front of the skull.

DELTOID Forms the top of each shoulder and gives the upper arms a wide range of motion.

PECTORALIS MAJOR The large, fan-shaped muscle covering each side of the upper chest.

RECTUS ABDOMINIS A long, flat muscle that runs down the center of the **abdomen**.

RECTUS FEMORIS One of four large muscles at the front of the thigh.

TIBIALIS ANTERIOR The main muscle at the front of the lower leg that contracts to bend the foot toward the shin.

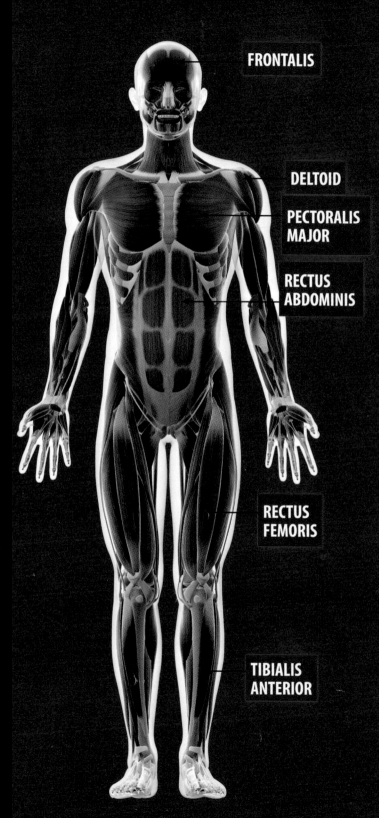

FRONTALIS

DELTOID

PECTORALIS MAJOR

RECTUS ABDOMINIS

RECTUS FEMORIS

TIBIALIS ANTERIOR

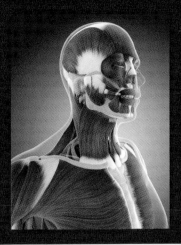

Face and Neck

Many different sets of muscles in the face and neck perform a variety of functions. Some muscles control the movements of sensory organs, such as the eyes, ears, and mouth. Some help the head move in different directions.

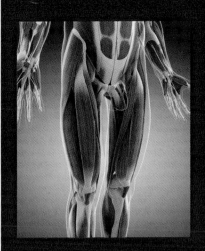

Upper Body

There are two types of muscles in the part of the body between the neck and the abdomen. Some are in the organs inside the ribcage. These include the cardiac muscle and muscles that help with breathing. Outside the ribcage, skeletal muscles assist movement in the arms, back, shoulders, and abdomen.

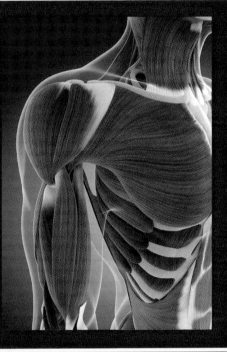

Leg

The limbs of the lower body include large, powerful muscles in the legs and very small ones in the toes. There are also muscles that move the joints at the **pelvis**, knee, and ankle. Along with helping a person move around, leg muscles support the entire body and keep it balanced.

Arm

From the shoulder to the wrist, there are strong muscles in both the upper arm and the forearm. Muscles in the forearm, between the elbow and wrist, control the hand and fingers. Muscles in the upper arm bend and extend the forearm. They are also attached to the shoulder muscles. The muscles of the shoulder, in turn, connect to the chest and upper back.

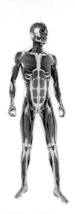

How Does the Muscular System Work?

Most skeletal muscles work by either pulling bones closer together or moving them apart. **Tendons** attach each end of a muscle to a bone. The places where a muscle attaches are called the origin and the insertion. The origin connects one end of the muscle to a bone that does not move. The insertion connects the other end to a movable bone. When the muscle contracts, it pulls the insertion toward the origin, bending the joint where the bones meet. However, after the muscle contracts, it cannot straighten out the joint again. For this reason, skeletal muscles work in pairs. One muscle of the pair, called the flexor, bends the joint. The other, called the extensor, straightens it.

The movements of skeletal muscles are voluntary. A person has to think about them for the brain and nervous system to make them happen. Smooth muscle movements are involuntary. These muscles contract and relax automatically, without the person thinking about them. When muscles contract, they produce heat. Even when a person is not moving, many muscles are making small contractions to keep the body at its normal temperature.

The Role of the Muscular System

MOVEMENT	Muscles help the body move.
POSTURE	Muscles make it possible to hold body positions.
TRANSPORT	Muscles move substances from one part of the body to another.
TEMPERATURE	Muscles help to generate body heat.

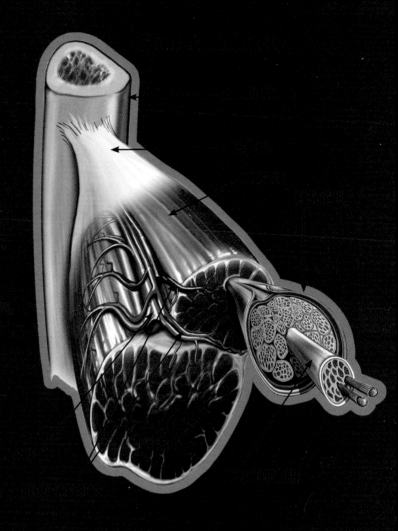

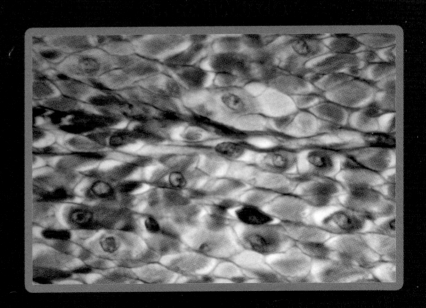

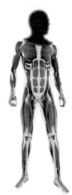

The Head and Neck

The human body has at least 80 muscles in the head and neck. The larger ones control the main movements of the head, such as turning and nodding. Smaller ones control movements of the eyes, mouth, nose, and ears. Muscles in the neck are connected to bones in the upper back, chest, and shoulders. These are some of the body's strongest muscles. They make the head able to move in all directions. They also hold the head up straight.

Making Faces

Muscles in the face are used to make any expression, from smiling or frowning to raising the eyebrows. Facial muscles are different from other skeletal muscles. Instead of connecting one bone to another, they connect bones to skin. These muscles pull on the skin of the face to move the lips, cheeks, and eyes. Six muscles around each eye can move it in eight different directions. Even more muscles inside the eye change the size of the **pupil** and adjust the **lens** to see clearly.

MUSCLES THAT MOVE THE NECK

The main muscles used for bending and turning the neck are attached to the base of the skull.

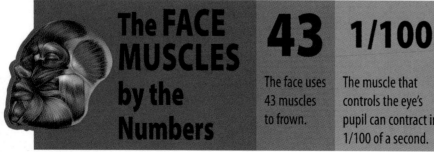

The FACE MUSCLES by the Numbers	**43**	**1/100**	**4**
	The face uses 43 muscles to frown.	The muscle that controls the eye's pupil can contract in 1/100 of a second.	The tongue has four sets of muscles to hold it in place.

Diagram of the Face

The muscles in the human face allow people to make more expressions than any other animal. Even the slightest expressions are noticeable because most facial muscles are just under the skin. Not everyone has exactly the same number of facial muscles, so some faces are more expressive than others.

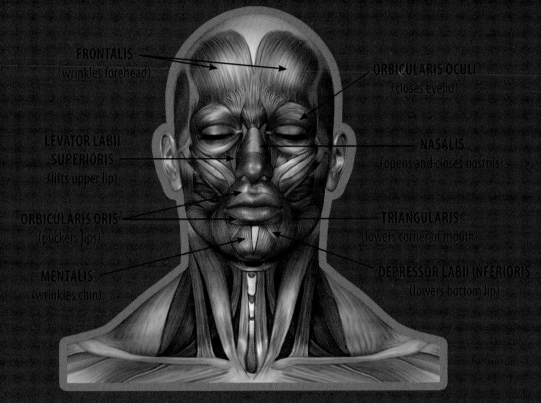

FRONTALIS
(wrinkles forehead)

ORBICULARIS OCULI
(closes eyelid)

LEVATOR LABII SUPERIORIS
(lifts upper lip)

NASALIS
(opens and closes nostrils)

ORBICULARIS ORIS
(puckers lips)

TRIANGULARIS
(lowers corner of mouth)

MENTALIS
(wrinkles chin)

DEPRESSOR LABII INFERIORIS
(lowers bottom lip)

Tongue Muscles

STYLOGLOSSUS
(raises the tongue)

HYOGLOSSUS
(lowers the tongue)

GENIOGLOSSUS
(moves the tongue forward and backward)

Eye Muscles

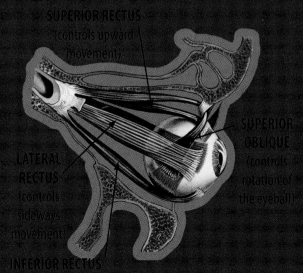

SUPERIOR RECTUS
(controls upward movement)

SUPERIOR OBLIQUE
(controls rotation of the eyeball)

LATERAL RECTUS
(controls sideways movement)

INFERIOR RECTUS
(controls downward movement)

The Chest, Back, and Abdomen

The trunk, or torso, is the main part of the human body. It includes the chest, back, and abdomen. It also contains many of the body's vital organs, including the heart, lungs, liver, and intestines. These organs are essential to life. A dome-shaped sheet of strong muscle divides the torso. It is called the diaphragm. The chest and upper back are above it. The abdomen and lower back are below it. The diaphragm controls pressure in the chest for proper breathing.

Large, fan-shaped muscles protect the upper chest, but they are used mainly to move the upper arms. The large muscles on each side of the lower back assist movement in the upper arms, too. Other muscles in the lower back move the spine and help the body stay balanced. Most of the upper back is covered by the large, flat trapezius muscles. They support the shoulders and move the shoulder blades.

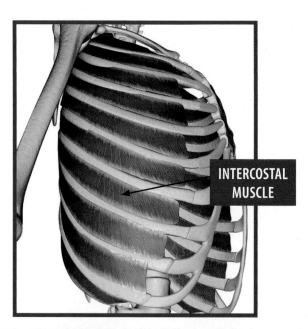

INTERCOSTAL MUSCLE

Small muscles between the ribs, called intercostals, work with the diaphragm to expand the chest as the lungs fill with air.

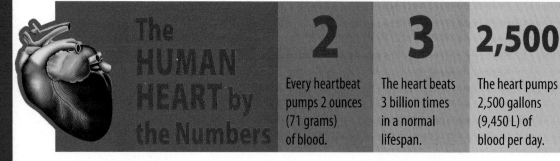

The **HUMAN HEART** by the Numbers

2	3	2,500
Every heartbeat pumps 2 ounces (71 grams) of blood.	The heart beats 3 billion times in a normal lifespan.	The heart pumps 2,500 gallons (9,450 L) of blood per day.

Diagrams of the Chest and Back

Nine different muscles in the upper chest and back control movements of the **humerus**. These muscles are important for extending and rotating the arms, as well as for reaching, pulling, swinging, and throwing. It is mainly muscles in the lower back and abdomen that move the torso itself.

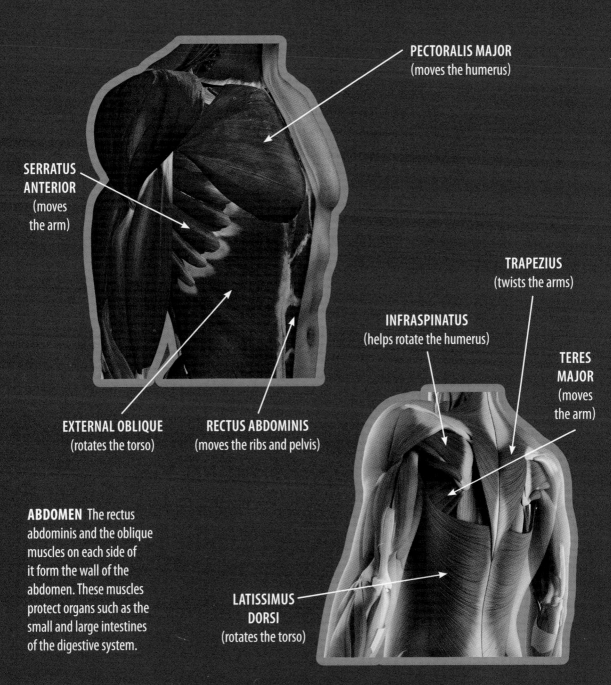

PECTORALIS MAJOR
(moves the humerus)

SERRATUS ANTERIOR
(moves the arm)

TRAPEZIUS
(twists the arms)

INFRASPINATUS
(helps rotate the humerus)

TERES MAJOR
(moves the arm)

EXTERNAL OBLIQUE
(rotates the torso)

RECTUS ABDOMINIS
(moves the ribs and pelvis)

ABDOMEN The rectus abdominis and the oblique muscles on each side of it form the wall of the abdomen. These muscles protect organs such as the small and large intestines of the digestive system.

LATISSIMUS DORSI
(rotates the torso)

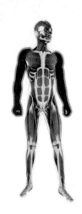

Arms and Hands

From the shoulder to the wrist, all the muscles in the arm work together to move the arm and hand. The biceps and triceps in the upper arm bend the elbow to raise the forearm toward the shoulder. These muscles work in pairs. As the biceps in front contracts, the triceps in back stretches and lengthens. When the triceps contracts, the biceps relaxes, and the elbow joint straightens.

Long tendons connect muscles in the forearm to the fingers. Muscles on the inside of the forearm bend the fingers. Those on the outside straighten them. Small muscles in the hand and fingers make them capable of delicate movements. Working with muscles in the arms, hands and fingers are also capable of great force, such as grabbing, gripping, and twisting.

Thumbs Up

Humans are the only animals with fully opposable thumbs. "Opposable" means that the thumb is able to turn in toward the other fingers. This allows the fingers to hold objects with a pinch-like grip.

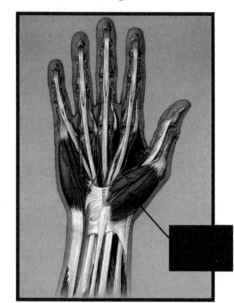

Three muscles, called thenar muscles, form the bulge at the base of the thumb and produce the fine movements of the thumb.

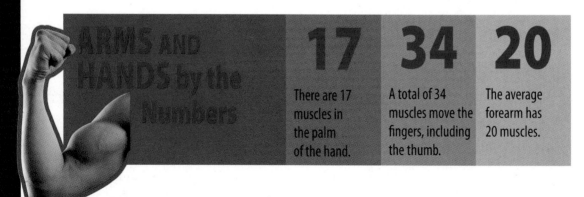

ARMS AND HANDS by the Numbers

17	34	20
There are 17 muscles in the palm of the hand.	A total of 34 muscles move the fingers, including the thumb.	The average forearm has 20 muscles.

Diagrams of the Arm

Although the human forearm has almost two dozen muscles, the upper arm has only four. Three of them, including the biceps, are in the front of the upper arm. The triceps muscle is the only one in the back.

Forearm Muscles

Upper Arm Muscles

PRONATOR TERES
(helps rotate
the forearm)

BRACHIORADIALIS
(helps rotate
the forearm)

TRICEPS

BICEPS

FLEXOR CARPI
RADIALIS
(helps bend
the wrist)

PALMARIS
LONGUS
(helps move the wrist)

FLEXOR CARPI ULNARIS
(helps bend the wrist)

BRACHIALIS
(connects the humerus
to the forearm)

Shoulder Muscles

The muscles of the shoulder
help connect the arm to
the rest of the body.

Legs and Feet

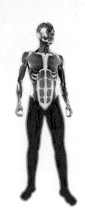

The thigh, or upper leg, starts at the gluteus maximus. This very strong muscle moves the thigh and helps the body rise from a sitting position. It is also important in climbing and walking up stairs. The sartorius muscle stretches across the thigh, from the outside of the hip to the inside of the knee. The sartorius bends the leg at the knee joint. It also turns the thigh sideways at the hip, which allows the body to sit, kneel, and kick.

The lower leg contains the soleus muscle. Located in the calf, or back part of the lower leg, it is the muscle that can pull with the greatest force. The soleus is important for walking and running, because it bends the ankle joint. The soleus, together with the gastrocnemius muscle, lifts the heel and rolls the foot onto its toes. The **Achilles tendon** attaches the lower part of the soleus muscle to the heel.

WORK YOUR MUSCLES

To stay strong and healthy, muscles need to move. One of the best ways to work muscles is weight-bearing exercise. Stretching muscles is important, too.

Aerobic exercise is a good way to work skeletal muscles. It also keeps the cardiac muscle strong. Any activities that increase heart rate and breathing are aerobic.

Diagrams of the Legs and Feet

Like the upper arm, the upper leg has a biceps muscle. Called biceps femoris, it is one of the three main muscles in the back of the thigh. The quadriceps femoris is the main group of muscles in the front of the thigh.

Leg Muscles

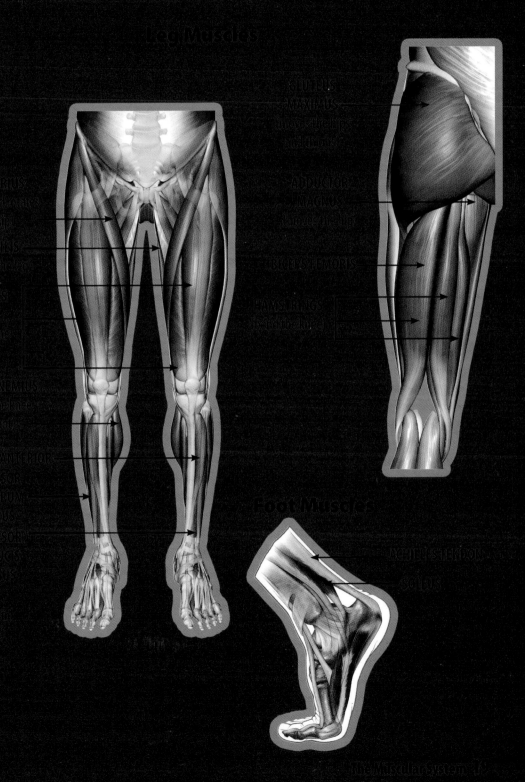

GLUTEUS MAXIMUS
(moves the hips and thighs)

SARTORIUS
(bends and rotates the hip)

ADDUCTOR MAGNUS
(moves the leg)

GRACILIS
(moves the leg)

BICEPS FEMORIS

QUADRICEPS FEMORIS
(straightens the knee joint)

HAMSTRING
(bends the knee)

GASTROCNEMIUS
(bends the knee and foot)

TIBIALIS ANTERIOR

EXTENSOR DIGITORUM LONGUS

EXTENSOR HALLUCIS LONGUS
(bends the foot)

(extend the toes)

Foot Muscles

ACHILLES TENDON

soleus

Keeping Healthy

Healthy muscles make the human body strong and flexible. Physical activity, getting enough rest, and eating the right foods are all important ways to take care of muscles. Healthy muscles also keep joints working properly and pain-free.

Exercise

When muscles are not used, they become weak. They need to be active. Any kind of movement is good, but **resistance** exercise is especially helpful for increasing muscle strength. Lifting weights is a well-known type of resistance exercise. **Calisthenics** and yoga use the weight of the body itself for resistance.

Relaxation

Resting muscles is as important as exercising them. Some gentle stretches are often all that is needed to relax tired muscles, but sleep is important, too. Some scientists believe that the body replaces muscle tissue more quickly during sleep. When muscles are strained or overused, adding **Epsom salts** to a hot bath may reduce soreness and aching.

Using weights for resistance can improve muscle strength in as few as two 30-minute sessions per week.

HIGH IN PROTEIN

MEAT

MILK

CHEESE

EGG

Protein-rich Foods
Eating foods with a great deal of protein helps to maintain and repair muscles. Meat, fish, and eggs are good sources. Milk and other dairy products, such as yogurt and cheese, also contain calcium, which helps muscles move properly.

9
main types of muscular dystrophy affect children and adults alike.

HIGH RISK
Only about 20% of people who develop ALS live more than five years.

Muscle Diseases

Many different diseases and medical conditions affect the muscular system. Fibromyalgia causes muscle pain, stiffness, and fatigue in different parts of the body. The cause is unknown, and there is no cure. Treatments include medications, exercise, and reducing stress.

Muscular dystrophy is a disease that can occur at any age and has no cure. It damages muscle fibers, causing severe weakness and stiffness. Over time, muscles stop functioning and waste away.

Amyotrophic lateral sclerosis, or ALS, is a disease that destroys nerves in the brain that control skeletal muscles. The body loses both strength and movement. In time, a person becomes unable to swallow and breathe. The illness is also known as Lou Gehrig's disease, after the baseball player of the 1920s and 1930s who was one of its victims.

Studying the Muscular System

Writings that survive today, known as the Edwin Smith Surgical Papyrus, show that people in ancient Egypt studied anatomy.

S everal types of physicians, or doctors, study and treat diseases of the muscular system. These present-day medical specialists include rheumatologists, orthopedists, and neurologists. However, people have been studying the muscles of the human body since ancient times.

In Scotland, William Balfour writes the first full description of fibromyalgia.

1816

ANATOMICAL MANUSCRIPT A

1830

Scottish anatomist Charles Bell first describes muscular dystrophy as a progressive, or steadily worsening, muscle weakness.

1510 and 1511 Italian scientist and artist Leonardo da Vinci produces a group of drawings called Anatomical Manuscript A. The detailed and accurate drawings show the anatomy, or structure, of the human body and the movements of muscles.

1970s

American chemist Paul Lauterbur develops nuclear magnetic resonance imaging, or MRI, technology, which is now commonly used to detect muscle diseases.

About 460 to 375 BC

The Greek physician Hippocrates, who is known as the "father of medicine," spends much of his life studying the human body.

About 335 to 280 BC

In Alexandria, Egypt, Herophilus of Chalcedon studies the human body, including the health benefits of gymnastics.

About 129 to 216 AD

Galen of Pergamum, a city in Greece, studies the human skeleton and surrounding muscles.

1672

The muscle disease myasthenia gravis is first recorded as a distinct medical condition by British physician Thomas Willis.

1543

Belgian physician Andreas Vesalius publishes *On the Fabric of the Human Body*, the first complete textbook on human anatomy.

1980s

Tissue engineering is developed, which allows doctors to repair or replace damaged muscle.

2007

The U.S. Food and Drug Administration approves the use of Lyrica, the first drug for the treatment of fibromyalgia.

Working Together

Without the muscular system, many other systems of the body could not function. Muscles and bones are constantly working together. In fact, these two systems are often called by one name, the musculoskeletal system. If bones were not connected to muscles, the human body would have no shape or movement.

Muscles Need Nerves

As much as bones need muscles, muscles need nerves. Without the nervous system to carry messages to and from the brain, muscles would not contract. Nerves pass through every muscle fiber. The fibers that are close to each other share nerve endings. Any action in the nerve endings sends energy into the fibers. The result is a contraction, which makes some part of the body move.

Smooth Moves

Smooth muscles do much of the work in many systems of the body. In the excretory system, the bladder is a muscular organ that stores urine. When the bladder contracts, it allows waste-containing urine to flow out of the body. In the digestive system, muscles in the large intestine help the body pass waste products.

After a meal or snack, smooth muscles automatically move food through the esophagus, the stomach, and the small intestine during the next six to eight hours.

Muscles and Breathing

Muscle cells, like all cells, need oxygen to stay alive. The respiratory system supplies the oxygen. Several muscles are important parts of this system. The diaphragm is the main one. When it contracts, it causes a person to inhale, or breathe in, oxygen-rich air. When it relaxes, other muscles force the body to exhale, or breathe out. This empties the lungs so that they can take in more oxygen.

Running is a good way to exercise the muscles of the respiratory system.

UNDER CONTROL

The part of the nervous system that controls skeletal muscles includes 31 pairs of nerves in the spine and 12 pairs in the brain.

50 TO 85%

of a person's maximum heart rate is a good target rate to reach during aerobic exercise.

More Than One

The heart is the main organ of the cardiovascular system. It is the body's hardest-working organ. Without cardiac muscle constantly pumping blood, a person cannot survive.

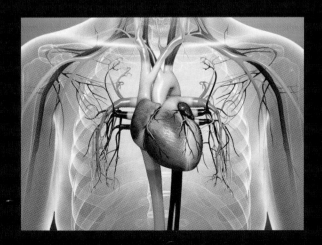

Careers

Several types of doctors and other health-care professionals specialize in treating muscular system problems. Many of these careers require a background in science, as well as an interest in working with and helping people. Before considering any career, it is important to research options and to learn about the educational requirements of the profession.

Physical Therapist

Education
- Bachelor's degree
- Master's or DPT degree
- Must be licensed

Tools

Weights

Physical therapists help patients of all ages improve movement and their ability to manage daily activities after an illness or injury. These therapists also help people cope with long-term pain or permanent physical disabilities. They teach patients exercises and other fitness activities to help their conditions. Therapists may also use techniques such as massage to relieve pain and improve muscle strength. Orthopedic physical therapists specialize in working with the musculoskeletal system, including muscles, bones, tendons, and **ligaments**. Physical therapists may work in hospitals, clinics, fitness centers, or sports organizations.

Education
To work as a physical therapist, a person must complete college and earn an advanced degree. This may be a master's degree or a DPT (doctor of physical therapy). Physical therapists also need to pass a national examination.

Rheumatologist

Most rheumatologists specialize in treating arthritis and other disorders that involve pain in muscles, bones, and joints. They try to help people manage constant pain and improve how their bodies function.

Education

Becoming a rheumatologist requires four years of medical school after college. Students also complete a three-year residency program, providing patient care under the supervision of an experienced physician. Then, they must pass a national exam and complete two or three years of advanced training.

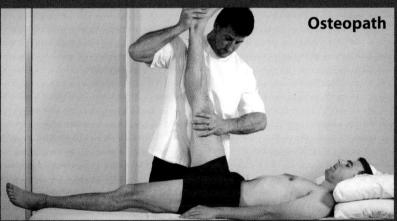

Osteopath

Osteopaths are doctors who treat pain and disorders of muscles, bones, and joints without drugs or surgery. They often use manual techniques, such as massage. They also advise patients about diet, exercise, and stress reduction to improve overall health.

Education

After earning a college degree, osteopaths complete four years of medical school. They earn a DO (doctor of osteopathic medicine) degree. They also spend 300 to 500 hours studying the musculoskeletal system and learning hands-on medical techniques. Many osteopaths then complete residencies.

The Muscular System Quiz

T est your knowledge of the muscular system by answering these questions. The answers are provided below for easy reference.

1 What is the longest muscle in the human body?

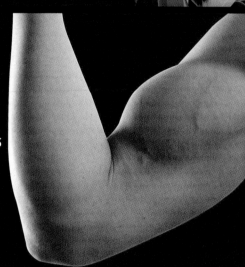

4 What pair of muscles bends and straightens the elbow joint?

7 In what year did Andreas Vesalius publish *On the Fabric of the Human Body?*

9 What is another name for amyotrophic lateral sclerosis (ALS)?

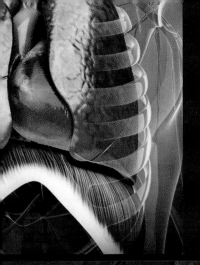

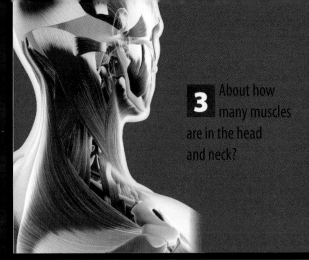

2 What dome-shaped sheet of muscle lies between the chest and the abdomen?

3 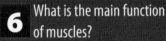 About how many muscles are in the head and neck?

5 How many types of muscles are in the human body?

6 What is the main function of muscles?

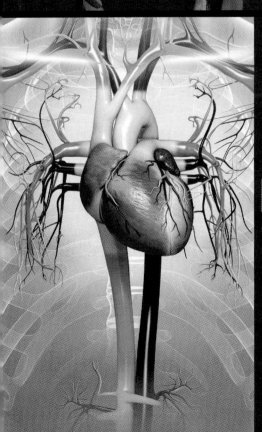

8 About how many times does the heart beat during a normal lifetime?

10 Where is the body's smallest muscle located?

Activity

To learn how flexor and extensor muscles work, bend and straighten your left elbow to move your forearm up and down. Use your right hand to feel how the biceps and triceps muscles in your upper arm work together.

MUSCLES IN ACTION

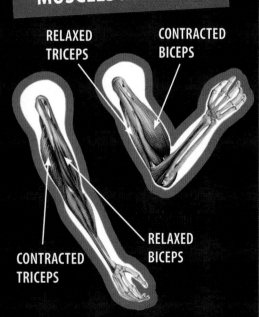

RELAXED TRICEPS

CONTRACTED BICEPS

CONTRACTED TRICEPS

RELAXED BICEPS

Checking Your Heart Rate

To learn how the cardiac muscle in your heart works, check your heart rate.

1 Press the index and middle finger of one hand lightly against your neck between the windpipe in the front and the large muscle on the side.

2 Adjust the position of the fingers until you feel a pulse. Each pulse is a heartbeat.

3 Count each time you feel the pulse for 10 seconds.

4 Multiply the number of pulses by 6 to calculate your heartbeats per minute.

5 Write down the number and label it "resting heart rate."

6 Now, start running in place or doing jumping jacks for 1 or 2 minutes. When you stop, repeat steps 1 through 4 to check your heart rate again.

7 Write down the number next to your resting heart rate to see how much faster your heart is beating after exercise.

When the body is physically active, the heart pumps faster to give muscles the extra blood and oxygen they need to keep moving.

Key Words

abdomen: the part of the body between the chest and the pelvis

Achilles tendon: the tendon that connects the calf muscles in the lower leg to the heel of the foot

calisthenics: exercises, such as sit-ups and push-ups, that are usually done without special equipment

contract: to become smaller or shorter

Epsom salts: salt-like crystals of the chemical magnesium sulfate that can be added to bathwater to soothe muscles

esophagus: the muscular tube through which foods and liquids travel from the mouth down to the stomach

fibers: long, cord-like cells

humerus: the bone in the upper arm between the shoulder and the elbow

lens: the part of the eye that focuses on what the eye sees

ligaments: short, strong bands that connect bones or hold joints together

organs: parts of the body that perform special functions

pelvis: the ring of strong bones that forms the hips

pupil: the opening in the center of the eyeball that controls the amount of light that enters the eye

resistance: involving an opposing force, or something that pushes back

striated: striped

tendons: strong bands that connect muscles to bones

Index

Log on to www.av2books.com

AV² by Weigl brings you media enhanced books that support active learning. Go to www.av2books.com, and enter the special code found on page 2 of this book. You will gain access to enriched and enhanced content that supplements and complements this book. Content includes video, audio, weblinks, quizzes, a slide show, and activities.

AV² Online Navigation

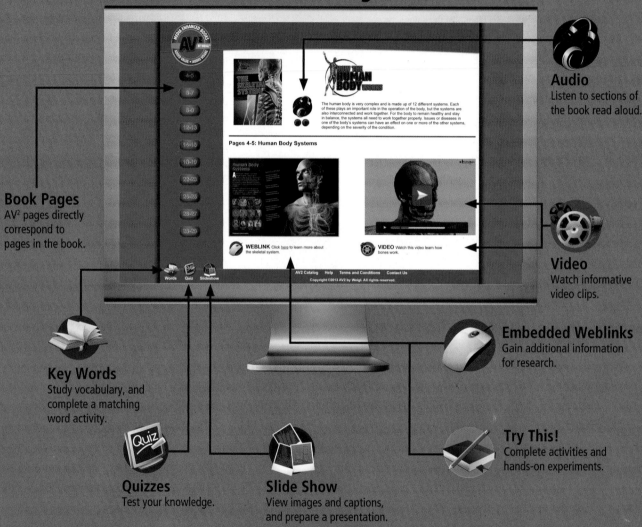

Audio
Listen to sections of the book read aloud.

Book Pages
AV² pages directly correspond to pages in the book.

Video
Watch informative video clips.

Key Words
Study vocabulary, and complete a matching word activity.

Embedded Weblinks
Gain additional information for research.

Try This!
Complete activities and hands-on experiments.

Quizzes
Test your knowledge.

Slide Show
View images and captions, and prepare a presentation.

AV² was built to bridge the gap between print and digital. We encourage you to tell us what you like and what you want to see in the future.

Sign up to be an AV² Ambassador at www.av2books.com/ambassador.